Flower Coloring Book
For Adults

FLOWER COLORING

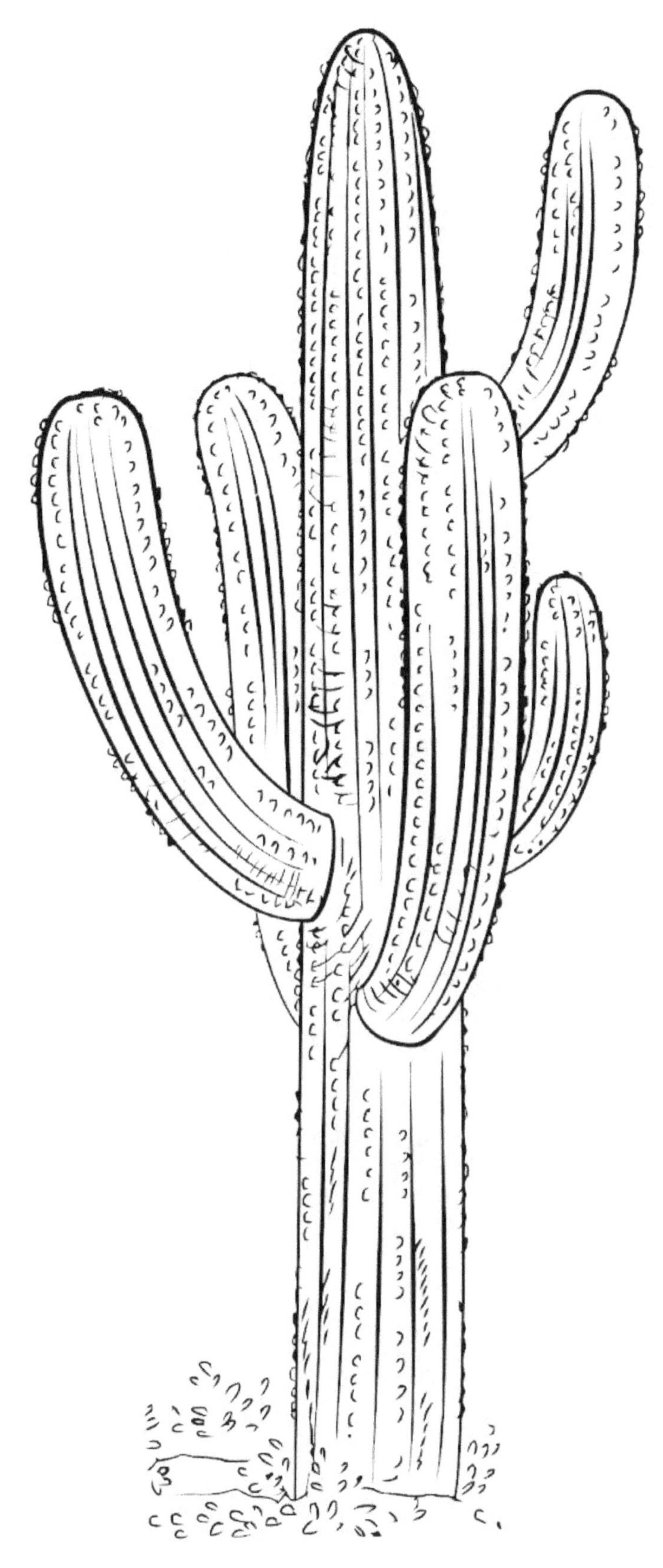

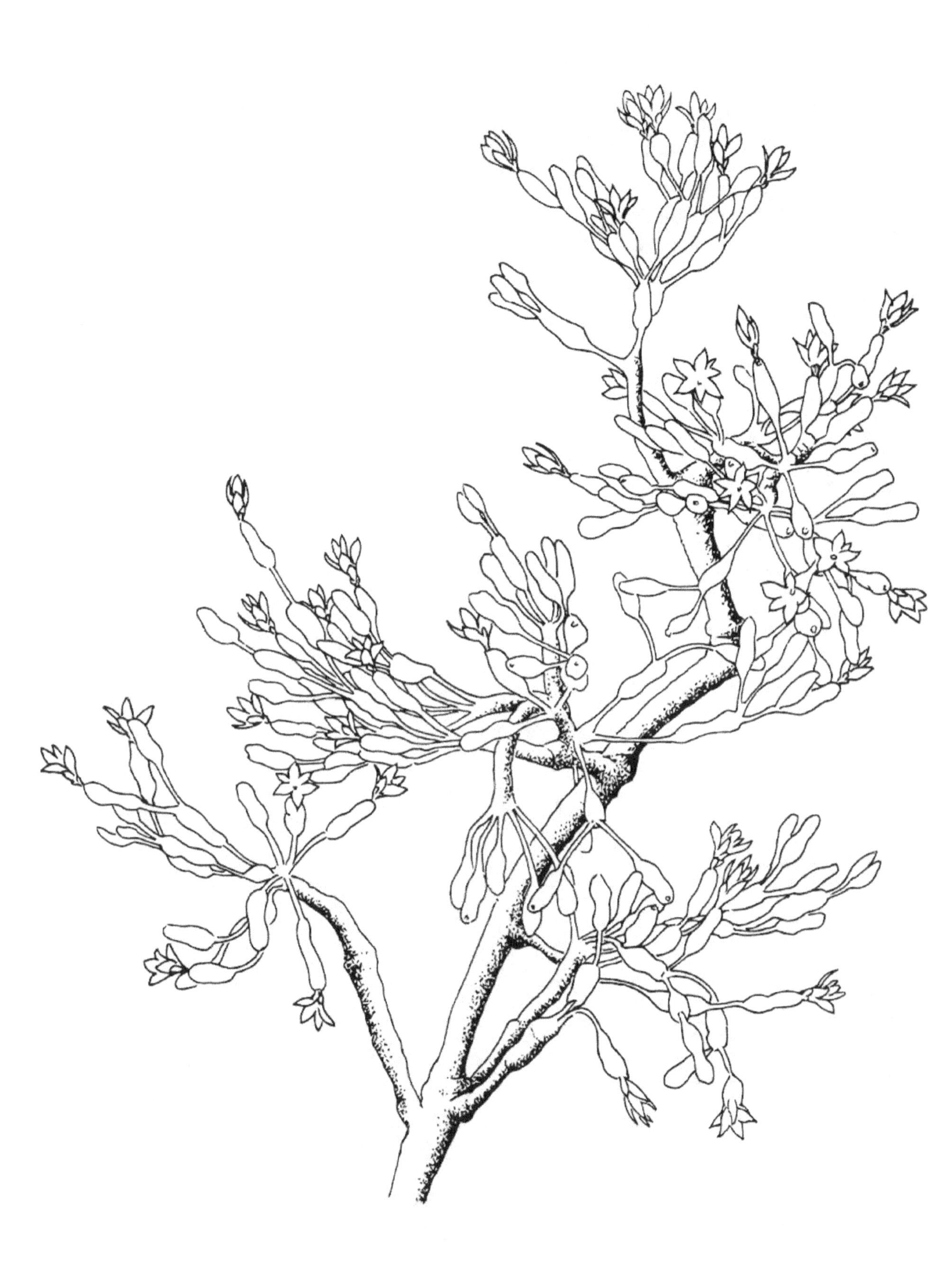

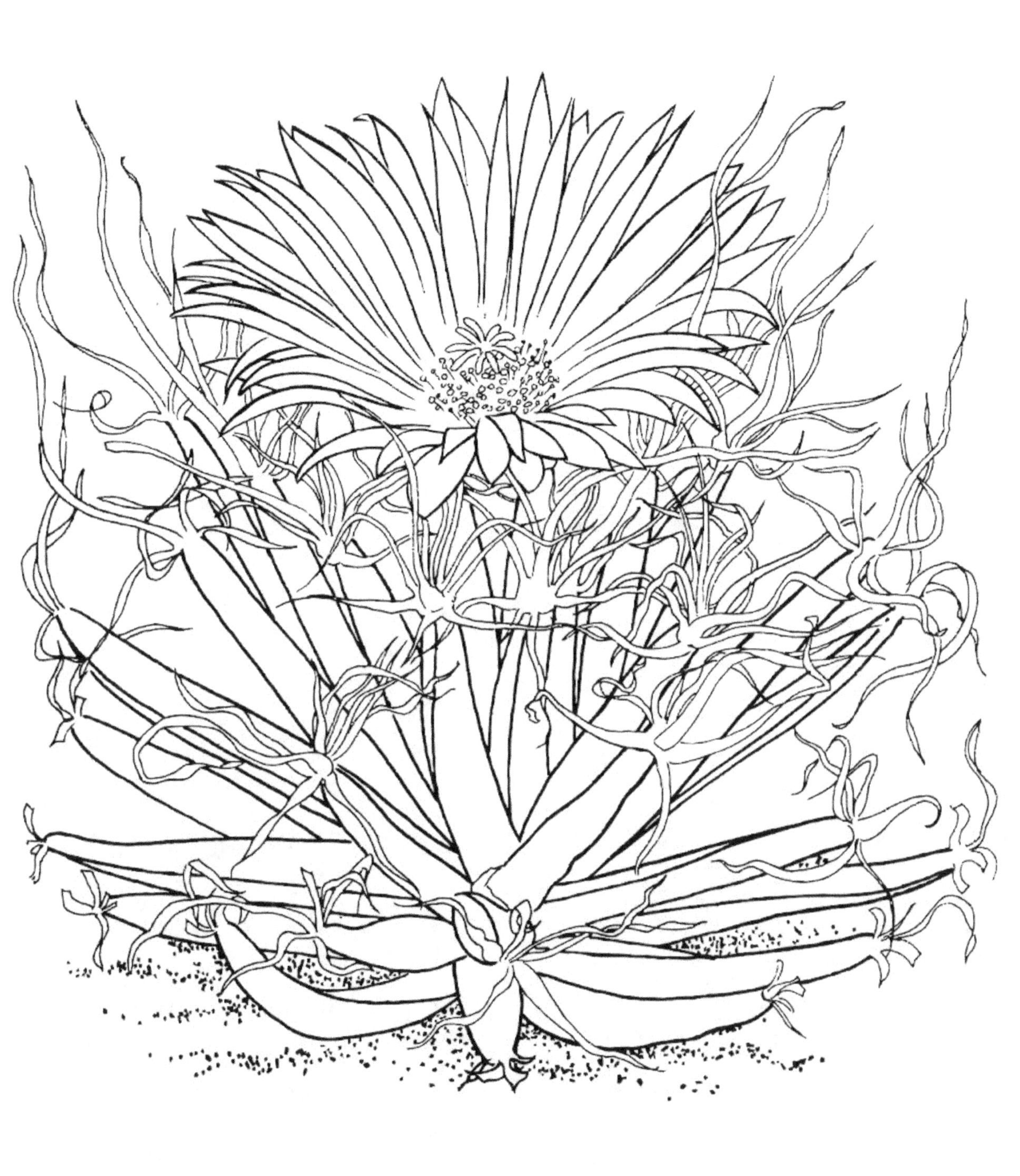

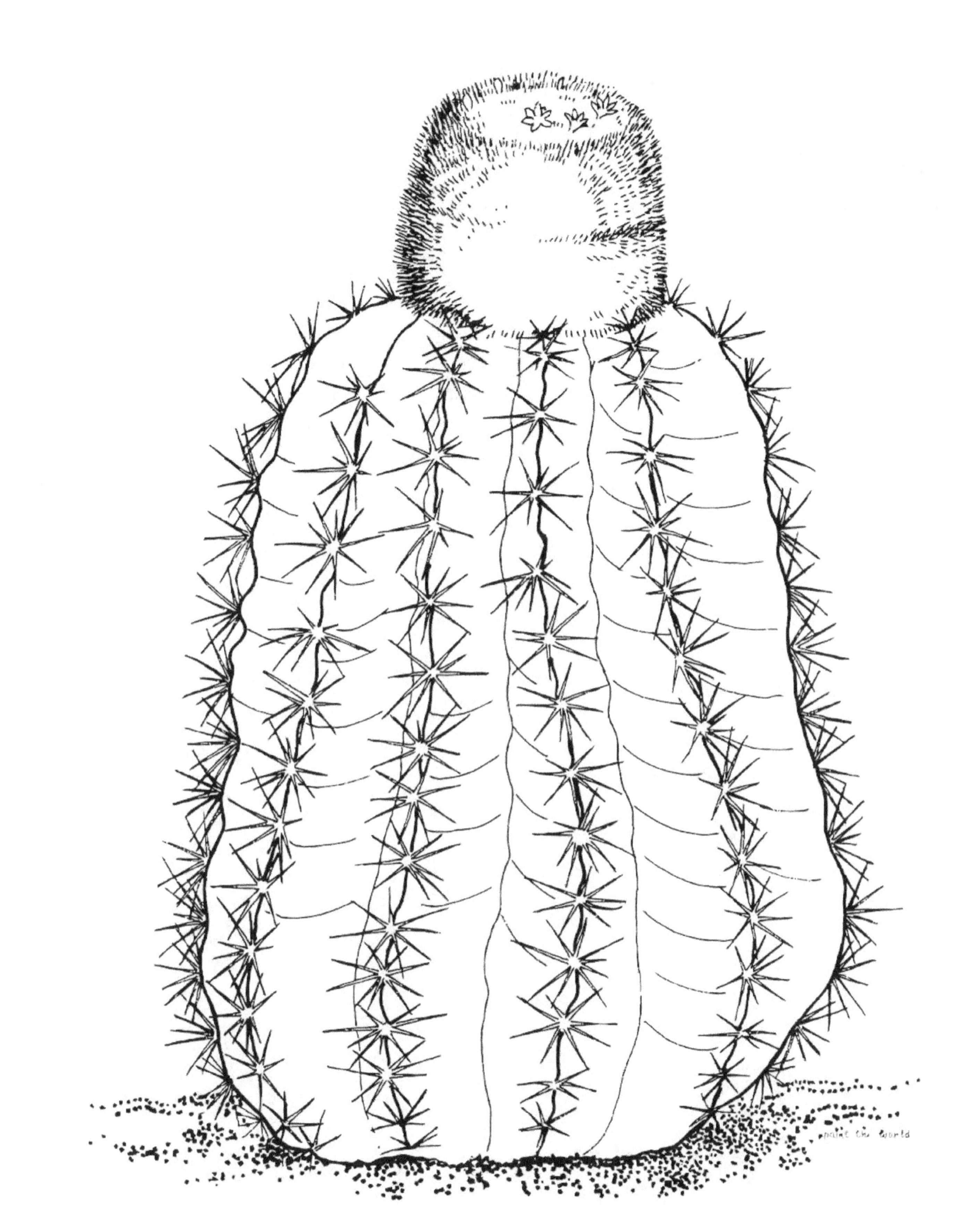
paint the world

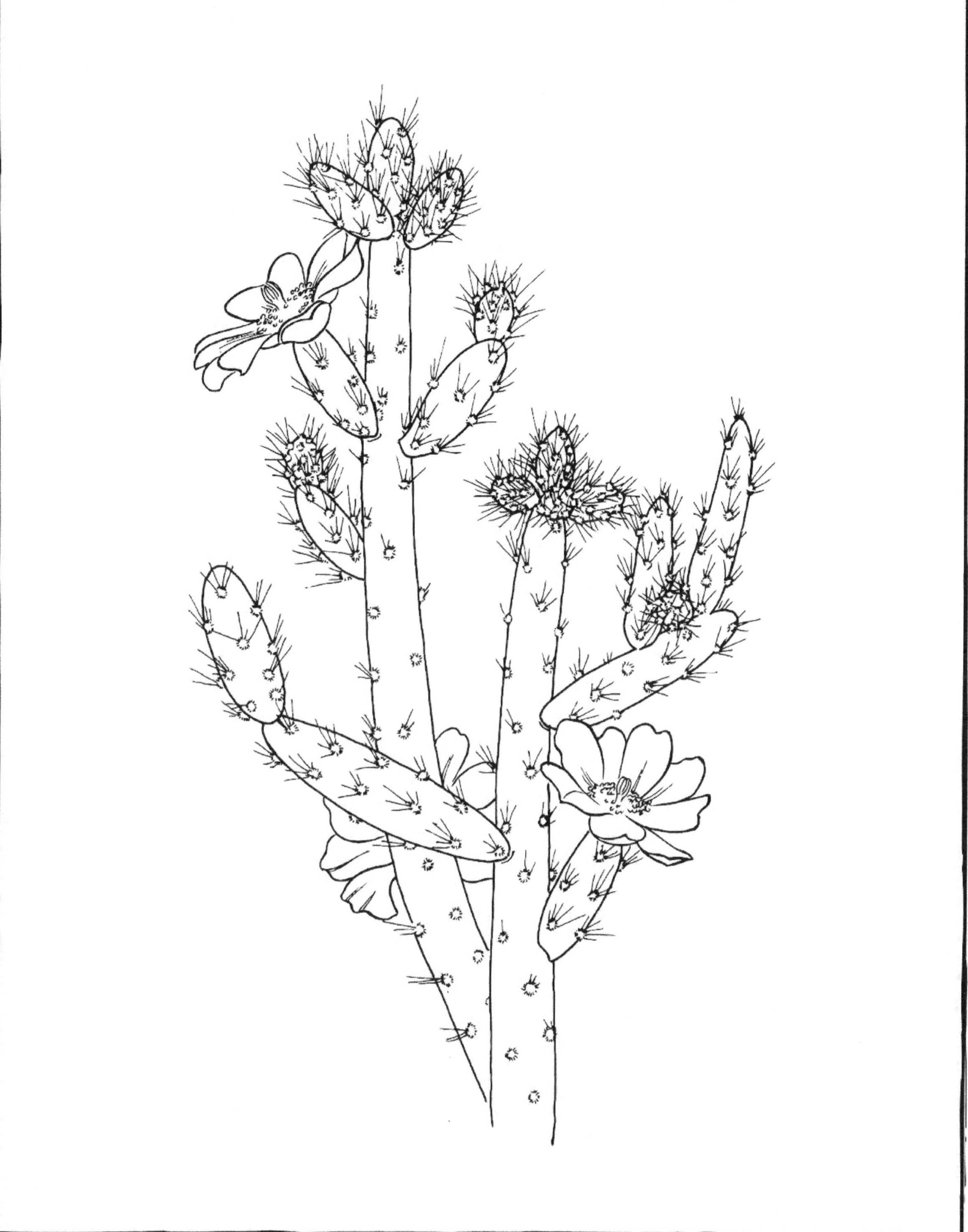

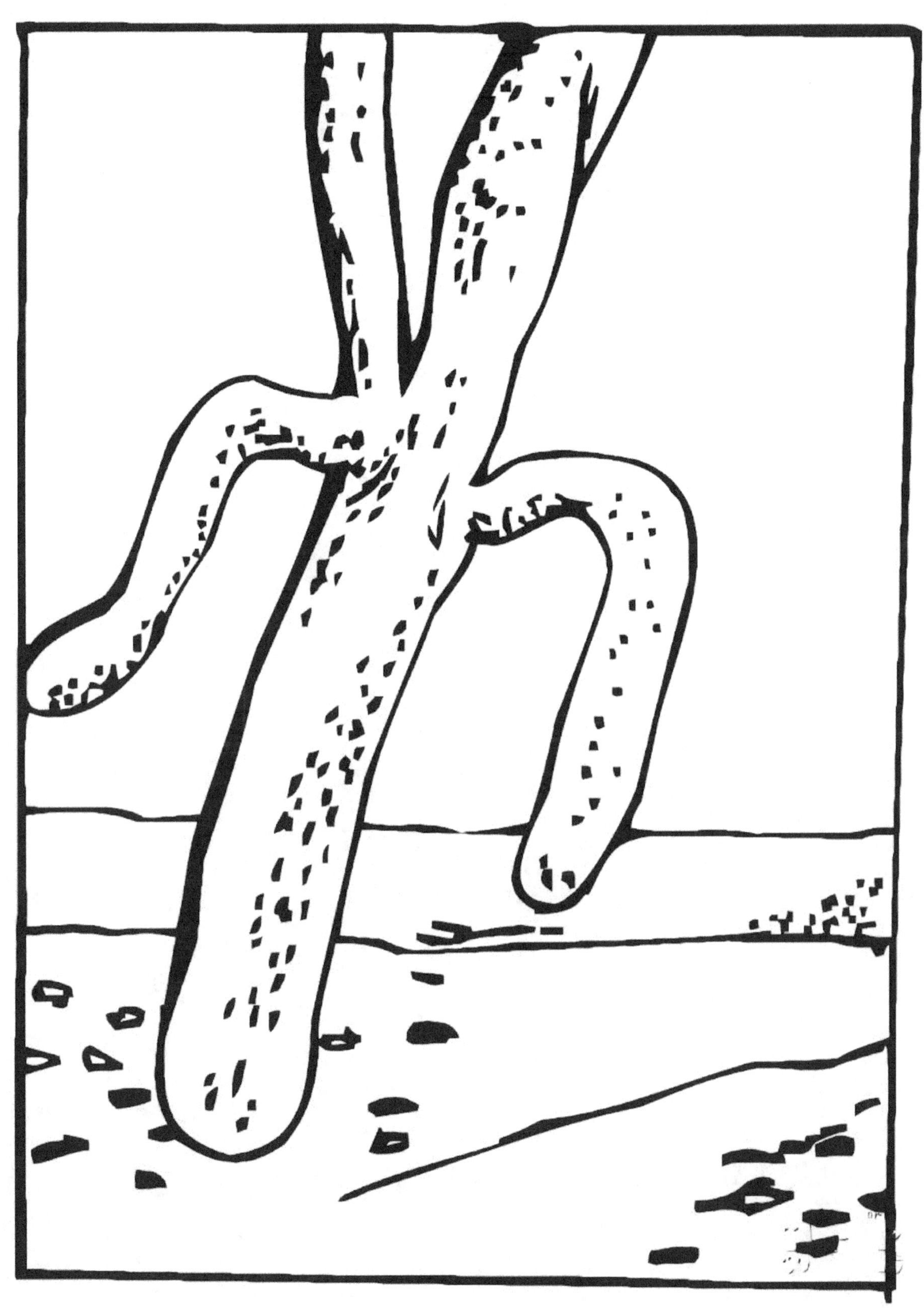

www.ingramcontent.com/pod-product-compliance
Lightning Source LLC
Chambersburg PA
CBHW081449250726
48662CB00009B/3005